Table of Contents

Introduction

In October 1993, the Quick Reaction Force Headquarters in Mogadishu, Somalia observed, "convoys are more vulnerable to attack than ground maneuver forces and should be planned and executed as a combat operation."[1] During the period from 1993 to 2012, every major United States Army operation confirmed this reality. Logistics forces conducting ground convoys suffered 17 percent, or 167 soldiers, of all Army personnel killed in action during both Operation Enduring Freedom and Iraqi Freedom between November 2001 and September 2010.[2] Whether high intensity as experienced during the March 2003 Iraq invasion or low intensity as seen during Operation Uphold Democracy in Haiti from 1994 to 1995, sustainment organizations maintained the enduring requirement to conduct supply distribution operations with armed convoy escorts. Assumptions exist, based on the enduring concept of AirLand Battle introduced in the 1980s with Field Manual 100-5, that the Army conducted convoys as a rear area operation and that the rear area is secure. Sustainment brigade doctrine, published in 2009, countered that claim, indicating that, "supply routes are assumed not be secure on a high threat area."[3] The asymmetric conflicts over the past 20 years were nonlinear and featured no rear area or front line.[4] The Army clearly entered an era requiring armed escorts to ensure convoy protection.

Doctrine, in the form of Field Service Regulations, dating back to 1917 recognized that infantry provided convoy security escort in a strength dependent upon the convoy's multiple

---

[1] Dean Dominique, "Gun Trucks: A Vietnam Innovation Returns," *Army Logistician* 38, no. 1 (January 2006): 47.

[2] Ad Hoc report from the Defense Manpower Data Center generated on March 13, 2012. The report listed all hostile casualties with their associated service, component, occupational specialty, and cause of death during Operations Iraqi Freedom and Enduring Freedom.

[3] Department of the Army, *Field Manual Interim 4-93.2 Sustainment Brigade* (Washington: Government Printing Office, 2009), B-58.

[4] Eyval Ziv, "Logistics In Asymmetric Conflicts," *Army Logistician* 44, no. 1 (January 2012): 46.

characteristics.[5] In a more modern context, doctrinal codification of convoy security escort remained undeveloped through minimal discussion in Field Manual 17-95, Cavalry Operations, and Field Manual 3-19.1, Military Police Operations.[6] Additionally, the Army's tactics doctrine, Field Manual 3-90, viewed convoy physical security consisting of a combination of organic security, escorts, and mobility corridors.[7] Over the last 20 years, incorporating external security capability with convoys strained both security forces and combat operations, forcing sustainment units to develop creative internal armed escort solutions similar to those seen in the Vietnam War.[8]

Wheeled vehicle modernization following the Vietnam War kept pace with other state-of-the-art platforms in the Army's ground fleet. However, the basic tables of organization and equipment failed to accommodate lessons learned resulting in transportation organizations with no internal armed security solution in 2012.[9] With modularity, the Army's transportation companies aligned under a multifunctional Combat Sustainment Support Battalion (CSSB) or a functional transportation battalion and created a distribution capability within sustainment brigades.[10] This configuration closed the distribution gap, in many cases, between theater supply and transportation via throughput down to the maneuver battalion level. Potentially crossing multiple divisional boundaries, a sustainment brigade was not limited by an area of operations

---

[5] War Department, *Field Service Regulation United States Army* (Washington: Government Printing Office, 1914, corrected to 1917), 65.

[6] Gregory Peterson, "Tactical Convoy Planning For Sustainers," *Army Logistician* 41, no. 5 (September 2009): 46.

[7] Department of the Army, *Field Manual 3-90 Tactics,* (Washington: Government Printing Office, 2001), B-72.

[8] Daniel Rossi, "The Logistics Convoy: A Combat Operation," *Army Logistician* 37, no. 1 (January 2005): 39.

[9] Everett Lacroix, "Adding MRAPs To Transportation Companies," *Army Sustainment* 43, no. 5 (September 2011): 26.

[10] Department of the Army, *Field Manual Interim 4-93.2 The Sustainment Brigade* (Washington: Government Printing Office, 2009), 2-91.

and supported more than one division.[11] The 3rd Corps Support Command, consisting of five sustainment brigades, conducted over 37,000 convoys throughout the theater during its yearlong deployment to Iraq from 2005 to 2006. Intense exposure to the road transpired with over 1,400 enemy engagements along protected supply routes.[12] The Army continued to conduct convoys and will likely face a similar threat for the unforeseeable future.

Operational planners faced four basic options regarding convoy security. They either resource security internally by sustainment brigades, or task external maneuver organizations, such as Army National Guard companies, host nation security forces, or private security companies. Nearly a decade of warfare in Iraq and Afghanistan demonstrated hundreds of examples with corresponding sets of risks accepted. The fundamental gap, however, is that sustainment brigades conducted armed escorted convoys and no Doctrinal, Organizational, Training, Materiel, Leadership, Personnel, or Facilities (DOTMLPF) solutions addressed how that integration occurs. To eliminate this problem, should the Army create dedicated armed convoy security escort capability within each sustainment brigade to enable self-securing distribution operations without external protection?

The thesis for this monograph posits, when externally resourced convoy escorts are used, then a sustainment brigade commander assumes risk with his distribution mission, and when internally resourced convoy escorts are constructed and employed, a sustainment brigade commander has complete control over convoy unity of command, home station training, and convoy cohesion.

This monograph examines multiple options available to operational level planners when considering and building theater distribution capability. Primarily, it focuses on the benefits and

---

[11] Ibid., 1-15.

[12] Brandon Cholek and Matthew Anderson Sr, "Distribution-Based Logistics In Operation Iraqi Freedom," *Army Logistician* 39 no. 2 (March 2007): 5.

shortfalls of both internal and external armed convoy escort. Additionally, it provides historical examples of convoy operations in asymmetrical environments and the associated security challenges. Finally, this monograph offers multiple convoy security solutions for operational planners, force managers, and the sustainment doctrine community to consider for review and implementation.

This study is important because the Army allowed arbitrary ad hoc convoy security solutions for over 30 years while not embracing the realities of the requirements in response to the emerging environment. The Army's distribution structure requires a sweeping shift to comprehensively close all gaps within its DOTMLPF architecture for sustainment organizations. This study extends the sustainment community's awareness of an ongoing problem and provides a solution. As U.S. Army Transportation Corps Historian Richard Killblane mentioned in 2005 after two years of intensive convoy operations in Iraq, Army units "took the protection and doctrine problem into their own hands."[13] The Army provided interim solutions in the form of Mine Resistant Ambush Protected (MRAP) vehicles to both Operation Iraqi Freedom and Operation Enduring Freedom; however, the lack of integration across the DOTMLPF remains. By identifying the problems and solutions within this monograph, leaders and planners within the Sustainment Center of Excellence, the Department of the Army G4, and operational level headquarters will have a better understanding of the problem and options available. The results of this study may contribute to emerging doctrine, force structure adjustments, materiel authorizations, and training improvements within the Army.

To avoid confusion, this study defines the meaning of terms associated with the problem statement. These definitions are necessary towards understanding the implications within the research and the recommendations.

---

[13] Richard Killblane, *Circle the Wagons: The History of US Army Convoy Security* (Fort Leavenworth: Combat Studies InstitutePress, 2005), 79.

Convoy: Joint and Army doctrine present Convoy in two very similar manners accepted as the standard for this monograph. First, in Joint Publication 1-02, *Department of Defense Dictionary of Military and Associated Terms,* convoy was simply, "A group of vehicles organized for the purpose of control and orderly movement with or without escort protection that moves over the same route at the same time and under one commander."[14] However, within the Army's interpretation, it is a "deliberately planned combat operation to move personnel and or cargo via a group of ground transportation assets in a secure manner to or from a target destination under the control of a single commander in a permissive, uncertain, or hostile environment."[15]

Convoy Escort: Simply put, convoy escorts protect a "convoy of vehicles from being scattered, destroyed, or captured."[16] Sustainment brigade doctrine references this term but fails to define it.

Additionally, this monograph references two subcategories of convoy escort: Internal Security and External Security. Internal Security encompassed organic assets—personnel and equipment—within an Army unit at the company, battalion, or brigade level. Planners and leaders organized those resources to accomplish their assignment mission with or without assistance from a higher headquarters or external organization. External Security comprised resources outside the sustainment brigade made available by a higher headquarters to accomplish the assigned mission. The external security enablers discussed in this monograph are Host Nation Support, Private Security Companies, and maneuver units outside the sustainment brigade's task organization.

Within the theoretical framework, AirLand battle doctrine from the 1980s drove how the Army operates in the 21st century. Specifically, rear area security existed, thus allowing freedom

---

[14] Department of Defense, *Joint Publication 1-02, Dictionary of Military Terms* (Washington: Government Printing Office, 2010, Amended Through 15 January 2012), 73.

[15] Department of the Army, *FieldManual 4-01.45 Tactical Convoy Operations* (Washington: Government Printing Office, 2009), 151.

[16] Department of Defense, *Joint Publication 1-02, Dictionary of Military Terms* (Washington: Government Printing Office, 2010, Amended Through 15 January 2012), 74.

of maneuver for convoys. This theory does not reflect the recent past, the current conditions, or much vision of the future environment. The past two decades illustrated proof that the rear area is subject to the same threat across the theater of operations. Sustainment brigades conducted convoys across all areas in a theater and regularly penetrated brigade combat team boundaries during throughput distribution operations. The current convoy security model within the current framework is nothing more than ad hoc armed escort through either internally or externally resourced assets. Joint and Army doctrine discussed aspects of incorporating convoy escorts into convoys, but does not codify any details.

There are six sections in this monograph. The first section included the background of the study, statement of the problem, purpose of the study, significance of the study, definition of terms, theoretical framework, research questions, and (proposed) thesis statement. The second section included the literature review discussing the theoretical framework and literature gaps. The third section included the research methodology followed by a fourth section, the case studies. The final two sections provided the findings, analysis, recommendations, and conclusion.

Literature Review

This section provides an understanding to the context justifying this monograph's research focus. Most research over the past two decades fixated on solutions that logistics units developed for their unique convoy security circumstances and requirements. Little discussion involved changes to convoy doctrine or to logistics unit personnel and equipment structure. Three themes examine the existing studies, models, and perspectives on this topic. This literature review applies a focused approach into internal convoy security, external convoy security, and status quo measures taken to create solutions in the combat environment. Key to each theme is the relevant application during the last 20 years of armed conflict requiring armed convoy operations. Lastly, it applies a level of critical thought by assessing the literature's focus, perspective, and audience.

Historical approaches to force protection disparities reached back to 1993 when Major Brian Layer saw the trend develop. He observed the unusual threats posed to wheeled vehicle convoys in asymmetrical environments. Specifically, he synthesized the connection between the 1993 version of Field Manual 100-5, *Operations*, and the operations other than war in both Somalia and Bosnia. Further, he recommended expanding both convoy and operations doctrine to meet the challenges of these emerging threats.[17] This effectively launched a series of discussions that would exceed two decades of armed conflict without a modicum of doctrinal or organizational improvement to resolve the problem.

More recently, the Army logistics community continued identifying numerous convoy protection solutions. Daniel Rossi, in 2005, and Julian Bond, in 2007, maintained the overarching linkage between convoys and combat. This connection, inherently tied to force protection enablers, elaborated on the basic gap between doctrinal reliance on military police to provide convoy security and the realities experienced during the Global War on Terror. Both authors advocated the addition of organic gun trucks to logistics unit's tables of organization and equipment.[18] Logistics convoys were simply unable to defend against asymmetrical threats while conducting what were clearly combat operations.

Codifying a doctrinal force protection level varied from conflict to conflict, but the guiding principles are the ratio of support vehicle to security vehicle. Lieutenant Colonel Frederick Godfrey, the senior logistics trainer at the Joint Multinational Readiness Center, attempted to establish a baseline for planning logistics convoys. His recommendations included having smaller convoys to ensure easier command and control, a mix of .50-caliber machine guns

---

[17] Brian Layer. "Some Principles of Convoy Operations In Operations Other Than War." Defense Technical Information Center. December 17, 1993. http://www.dtic.mil/cgi-bin/GetTRDoc?AD=ADA288865 (accessed April 1, 2012), 37.

[18] Daniel Rossi, "The Logistics Convoy: A Combat Operation," *Army Logistician* 37, no. 1 (January 2005): 40.

and 40mm automatic grenade launchers, and a density of at least three ground security vehicles to secure a 10-12 vehicle convoy with one additional security vehicle for every three additional logistics vehicles.[19] However, standardizing the security vehicle requirement is difficult as observed by Captain Julio Reyes in 2010. His forward support company in 2nd Infantry Brigade Combat Team, 82nd Airborne Division conducted convoy operations supporting humanitarian aid, assistance, and disaster relief missions. Movement required a security posture of two escort vehicles including two armed soldiers in the back of cargo trucks.[20] His limitations were the number of wheeled platforms available and threat assessment during the operation, but ultimately there were not enough soldiers for sustained operations. Finally, Lieutenant Colonel Gregory Peterson, a logistics trainer at the National Training Center addressed the gap between sustainment field manuals and security escort missions as recently as 2009. Inherently, logistics units will always conduct convoys as a core mission. Peterson identified that while some logistics doctrine may discuss tactics, techniques, and procedures, nothing exists to show how to coordinate and incorporate security into a convoy.[21]

Internal Convoy Security

Logistics units, in response to the operating environment, developed multiple convoy security solutions. In a self-proclaimed paradigm shift, the 68th Combat Sustainment Support Battalion reorganized its 360th Transportation Company. Major John Ruths explained in 2010 that the creation of the convoy security detachment (CSD) allowed the battalion to independently

---

[19] Frederick Godfrey, "The Keys To A Successful Combat Logistics Patrol,"*Army Logistician* 38, no. 4 (July 2006): 29.

[20] Julio Reyes, "Forward Support Company Operations In Haiti,"*Army Sustainment* 42 no. 4 (July 2010): 7.

[21] Gregory Peterson, "Tactical Convoy Planning For Sustainers," *Army Logistician* 41, no. 5 (September 2009): 47.

support a brigade combat team.[22] Other support battalions, such as the 204th Brigade Support Battalion in the 2nd Heavy Brigade Combat Team, 4th Infantry Division, created and trained similar CSD's to provide security for logistics convoys.[23] The battalion used mobile training teams to certify the element and ultimately employed the CSD during the brigade's National Training Center rotation and in support of Operation Iraqi Freedom.

Adding complexity to the ad hoc solutions was the Host Nation Trucking (HNT) option. As Major Michael Harris, a former Operations Officer for the 45th Sustainment Brigade, observed, HNT typically caused convoys to miss external security linkups orchestrated in cross-battlespace coordination.[24] The use of HNT or even host nation forces clearly added another strain on an already stressed enabler. The lack of reliability essentially unhinges most practical consideration of host nation resources within logistics convoys.

In early 2006, Major Dean Dominique, a transportation battalion executive officer, recommended the application of the Vietnam War gun truck concept.[25] With a lack of Army-provided protection platforms, units began creating gun trucks with makeshift armor and weapons mounts to merely protect themselves and deter attacks. This experience indicated that if the United States Army does not provide units and soldiers with the materiel needed to accomplish missions, pure creativity surfaces and ad hoc solutions arise.

Specialist Dustin Perry reported of struggles and shortfalls experienced by the Army National Guard's 1451st Transportation Company in 2007. The company, charged with transporting supplies in Iraq, suggested that successful convoys and convoy security can come

---

[22] John Ruths, "A Paradigm Shift At NTC: CSSBs That Think "Inside the Box," *Army Sustainment* 42, no. 3 (May 2010): 6.

[23] Michael Siegl, "Sustaining A BCT In Southern Iraq," *Army Sustainment* 42, no. 6 (November 2010): 29.

[24] Michael Harris and Eric Roby, "Echelons-Above-Brigade Convoy Management In Afghanistan," *Army Sustainment* 42, no. 6 (November 2010): 16.

[25] Dean Dominique, "Gun Trucks: A Vietnam Innovation Returns," *Army Logistician* 38, no. 1 (January 2006): 46.

from several elements within an organization. Specifically, the company pulled personnel from across the National Guard, to include infantrymen, cooks, military intelligence, and medics to assemble the convoy security element. The unit's security platoon leader, First Lieutenant Jacob Siegel, epitomized the entire concept of ad hoc convoy security with his statement, "It's a whoever-you-could-find-to-do-it mission."[26]

Many support battalions established their own tactics, techniques, and procedures for convoy security. One perspective, however, is the cost to the overall logistics mission when creating an internal security capability. The 26th Brigade Support Battalion, supporting the 2nd Heavy Brigade Combat Team, 3rd Infantry Division, developed a security platoon blueprint in 2006 as the standard for personnel and equipment. The battalion's "bend but don't break" approach required a generally high operating tempo supported by 50 soldiers.[27] When five of the nine organic companies organize under external supported maneuver battalions, that reduces the battalion to 419 personnel across three functional logistics companies and a headquarters company. Dedicating 50 personnel for a convoy security mission reduces a supply, maintenance, or health services capability not replaceable across the battalion.

External Convoy Security

From the perspective of an Army National Guard battalion charged with providing logistics convoy escort, Major Kris Kough's "Share the road: Convoy Escort" article in *Army Sustainment Magazine* in 2010 exhibited a common external security trend. Command and control for large and complex convoys became increasingly difficult when military vehicles combined with civilian contractor vehicles and third-country national trucks.[28] The challenges of

---

[26] Perry, *Hodgepodge' Convoy Escort Platoon Comes Together To Get Job Done,* http://www.nationalguard.mil/news/archives/2007/02/022007-Hodgepodge.aspx (accessed April 11, 2012).

[27] Timothy Page and Mark Weinerth, "Top Flite: How One BSB Secured Logistics Convoys in Iraq," *Army Logistician* 41, no. 3 (May 2009): 31.

[28] Kris Kough, "Share The Road: Convoy Escort," *Army Sustainment* 42, no. 3 (May 2010): 24.

secured and non-secured communications between vehicles along with an inadequate density of gun trucks providing security limited a convoy commander's ability to react effectively when leading these large, diverse convoys.

Douglas Macgregor saw this as the Army "designing itself to do what it wants to do, not what the strategic environment is demanding of it" and he subsequently argued the global trends required a radically different approach to security.[29] From a military point of view, Lieutenant Colonel Shawn P. Walsh's organization, a fuel battalion in Iraq consisting of seven fuel transportation companies, faced convoy security requirements despite the organic resourcing of only two ring mounts per company for crew-served weapon systems.[30] Concurrently, the lack of military police and other external security forces did not exist resulting in crude solutions during a time the Army claimed it was transforming.

Status Quo Convoy Security

Recommendations continued to spread throughout the sustainment community despite Operation Iraqi Freedom ending in 2010. In 2011, Everett Lacroix suggested the addition of Mine Resistant Ambush Protected (MRAP) vehicles to transportation companies.[31] The MRAP's 94 percent survivability rate is the basis of his argument. Additionally, Lacroix is among the first to publicly acknowledge the shortfalls associated with external convoy security. His analysis clearly laid out the benefits of unity of command, improved training proficiency and opportunities, and increased crew familiarity.

Richard Killblane's comprehensive historical examination of convoy security furnished the logistics community with a solid base of lessons to develop future solutions. He reinforced the

---

[29] Douglas Macgregor, *Transformation Under Fire : Revolutionizing How America Fights* (Westport: Prageger, 2003), 4.

[30] Shawn Walsh, "More Tooth For The Tail: The Right Stuff For CSS Operations,"*Army Logistician* 36, no. 1 (January 2004): 11.

[31] Everett Lacroix, "Adding MRAPs To Transportation Companies," *Army Sustainment* 43, no. 5 (September 2011): 26.

idea that the Army needs both gun truck doctrine and convoy security doctrine.[32] Eyal Ziv supported that argument in 2012 by balancing the notion of logistics convoys operating in a rear area behind combat forces during a conventional fight, but operating directly in contact with hostile forces during low intensity conflict. Ultimately, she asserts that the fundamental premise is that logistics forces need to protect themselves from enemy attacks.[33] Both authors understood the historical context and modern ramifications of not securing logistics organizations. However, neither indicated a preference for internal or external security, but rather some form of protection.

This monograph examined three fundamental hypotheses. First, when a commander uses internally resourced convoy security, then he assumes risk to sustainment capability and mission support. Second, when a commander uses externally resourced convoy security, then he assumes risk to training management, manning, synchronization, materiel, and standardization. Finally, when a commander accepts the status quo for convoy security, then he continues to pull resources out of hide while simultaneously implementing external assets when resourced from a higher headquarters.

From a very simple theoretical stance, the Army's difficulty embracing "form follows function" is clear. Over 20 years of conflict in a complex environment, threats continued to emerge and the connection to past lessons blurred. Many authors indicated the challenges and reality of this environment and the significant shortfalls in organization, equipment, and basic doctrine. While the Army claimed to have transformed, it did so only in name and not in practical application. Logistics units continued to develop ad hoc solutions to enduring problems where the only real solution is a radical shift in organization, equipment, and doctrine.

---

[32] Richard Killblane, *Circle the Wagons: The History of US Army Convoy Security* (Fort Leavenworth: Combat Studies Institute Press, 2005), 82.

[33] Eyval Ziv, "Logistics In Asymmetric Conflicts," *Army Logistician* 44, no. 1 (January 2012): 47.

Methodology

This monograph's methodology used a qualitative approach to test the form follows function theory. The theory predicted that removing function from an organization resulted in effectively removing its foundation, or form. As it applied to sustainment organizations, the basic function of conducting convoys with armed security escort required organizational structure to support the mission. Through an analysis of specific operations from 1992 to 2010, this study identified specific trends and shortfalls that created the gap between the function of sustainment organizations and the form used to conduct armed convoys. Therefore, two case studies serve to reinforce one another. The case studies are Operation Restore Hope and Continue Hope in Somalia from 1992 to 1994 and Operation Iraqi Freedom in Iraq from 2003 to 2010. Both cases allowed for a comparative view into the United States Army's operational environment for convoy operations.

Structured Focused Comparison

This study relied on the method and logic of structured, focused comparison to examine the two case studies. This structured comparison required the researcher to create general questions reflecting the research objective and discover the answer as applicable to each case study under examination.[34] This guided and standardized the systematic data collection, thereby making possible the comparison of the findings in each case. Additionally, as a focused comparison, it only dealt with specific characteristics and aspects of each historical case. This focus ensured a level of specificity while also yielding generic knowledge. The focused method ensured the researcher undertook the comparison with a theoretical focus and specific objective in mind.

Case Selection

---

[34] Andrew Bennett and Alexander Bennett, *Case Studies and Theory Development In The Social Sciences* (Cambridge: MIT Press, 2005), 5.

The case studies are Operation Restore Hope and Continue Hope in Somalia from 1992 to 1994 and Operation Iraq Freedom in Iraq from 2003 to 2010. Both cases encompassed operations supporting a balance across the spectrum of conflict to include unstable peace, insurgency, and general war. Each case allowed a distinct perspective into the approaches taken by planners and commanders towards the execution of ground convoys across various high and low intensity threats. For example, the Army's involvement in Somalia from 1992 to 1994 happened after a major combat operation, Operation Desert Storm in 1991, and set the stage for the reality of the non-contiguous battlefield and unconventional threats the Army faced. Operation Restore Hope confirmed that rear area security, as visualized in AirLand doctrine, was not realistic. The invasion of Iraq in March 2003 displayed the Army's overwhelming dominance of ground warfare and quickly defeated Saddam Hussein's forces in general war. General war, however, quickly shifted to counterinsurgency with a high intensity threat requiring ground forces to simultaneously respond and adapt structure, materiel, and tactics, techniques, and procedures to this emerging threat.

Questions

Six questions guided the case study analyses of logistics convoy security. Each question provided value as it nested within the research objective and focused on the theoretical approach. This research used the following questions to focus the comparison both across and within cases:

1) Did the operation have an overall force protection policy for ground movement? This question examines guidance directed to all ground forces within the theater and the corresponding requirements for vehicles, manning, and weapons platforms.

2) Did convoys have the required materiel to meet the force protection policy's requirements? This question reviews the vehicle and weapon platform response from the previous question and determines if adequate materiel was available for ground forces.

3) What was the average force protection to sustainment vehicle ratio? This question examines the density of vehicles providing armed convoy escort with the density of sustainment vehicles within logistics convoys.

4) How many casualties resulted from sustainment organization-led convoys?

5) What training did sustainment organizations conduct to prepare for convoys? This question examines the pre-deployment training conducted by deployed units to each operation. Additionally, it considers the context of tactics, techniques, and procedures along with convoy doctrine during that specific training period.

6) Who provided armed security for sustainment convoys? This question discovers the sources of armed security escort for sustainment convoys in each operation. Convoys have internally, externally, or hybrid resourced armed escort.

Sources

Sources for the case studies came from the expansive body of primary and secondary material. This includes professional journal articles, books, field manuals, and monographs. Additionally, the author conducted personal interviews with two former company commanders who served in Somalia. The author presented each interviewee with questions related to their organization's specific experience during preparation for deployment and actual combat operations. Each interview was conducted as an oral history interview and adhered to Army policies of informed consent in compliance with federal law. Collectively, there are sufficient sources available to research and analyze each case.

Convoys During Operations Restore Hope and Continue Hope

In April 1992, the United Nations issued UN Security Resolution 751 authorizing observers and peacekeepers to protect humanitarian aid workers in the northeastern African country of Somalia. Focused on safeguarding the delivery of supplies and relief, the mission later involved over 25,000 American soldiers in the form of Operations Restore Hope and Continue

Hope. By March 1994, 43 soldiers were dead and 153 wounded as the mission ended through a phased withdrawal.

The purpose of this section is to identify the operation's impact on ground convoys as conducted during a peacekeeping mission. This specific case study exposed the first enemy employment of the improvised explosive device and demonstrated the lack of protection that late 20th century Army vehicles provided to logistics and other non-armored units. This period began to shed light on this monograph's fundamental problem: logistics convoys do not operate solely in protected rear areas and are subject to the same enemy as conventional maneuver forces.

Operations Restore Hope and Continue Hope both offer great evidence to support the evolution of armed convoys as a core competency for the Army. Not only were logistics units charged with providing sustainment to American and coalition forces throughout the area of operations, they also supported the transportation efforts that moved tens of thousands of tons of humanitarian relief supplies from the ports in Mogadishu to the nine humanitarian relief sectors. The poorly maintained Somali road network and uncertainty of bandits attacking convoys added to the challenges faced by nearly all units.

The mission also served as a forcing function for the Army to realize its armored wheeled vehicle shortfalls. After a 50-pound improvised explosive device killed four military policemen in August 1993, the Army quickly developed and rapidly fielded add-on-armor kits and the first 50 M1114 Up-Armored Humvee vehicles, primarily to military police and scouts. This initiative, coupled with significant route security and convoy escort requirements, facilitated doctrinal developments for convoys to endure land mines, improvised explosive devices, snipers, and roadblock ambushes—problems not experienced since the Vietnam War.

The United States intervened in late 1992 following months of United Nation's relief efforts failing to meet humanitarian aid requirements. An estimated 20 percent of food relief was reaching the people who needed it and 25 percent of Somalis died due to starvation or disease.

With 14 clans competing for national power, none was strong enough to bring the country together and reduce the human suffering.

In what became the first of two intervention phases, Operation Restore Hope lasted from December 9, 1992 to May 4, 1993. On December 9, 1992, 1,800 Marines and Special Operations Forces arrived in Mogadishu to restore food distribution and humanitarian assistance operations. By early January 1993, over 500 Marines engaged in a shoot-out with Mohamed Farrah Aidid's forces in Mogadishu with 15 Somalis captured and no American casualties. Two weeks later, the United States sustained its first casualty when a Marine died while on patrol. That same week, the U.S. troop strength hit its peak of 25,800 and the United Nations presence reached over 38,000 soldiers from 23 nations supporting 49 relief agencies.

As the intervention transitioned into its second phase, Operation Continue Hope, violence and clashes with Aidid's bandits would characterize the bulk of the 11 months phase from April 1993 to March 1994. Units from the 10th Mountain Division conducted operations in Mogadishu with three major battles in the month of June. By August, bandits adjusted their techniques and began emplacing roadside mines at night—a period when the force protection policy restricted any military presence patrols. Four military policemen died because of a command-detonated improvised explosive device. In late August and early October 1993, Special Operations Forces conduct raids to capture Aidid. The October 3 raid results in 18 American Rangers killed in action and another 78 wounded.

A week following the Battle of Bakhara Market, Aidid declared a total cease-fire and President William J. Clinton barred any form of retaliation. Although over 5,000 U.S. reinforcements arrived in October, the UN Security Council called off the search for Aidid in November. By March 1994, all American forces departed and within 12 months, all United Nations forces withdrew. Somalia still lacked a functioning government.

Force Protection Policy

Did the operation have an overall force protection policy for ground movement? As early as December 1992, the force protection policy required a minimum of two vehicles per convoy.[35] However, during the first six months, no policy required convoys to consist of armored vehicles, combat arms unit escort, or any minimum crew served weapons. In mid-1993, the coalition forces terminated night patrols to reduce ambush threats.[36] This directive, unfortunately, allowed the enemy freedom of maneuver at night to emplace mines and improvised explosive devices.[37] Aware of coalition force's rules of engagement limitations, the Somali rebels were able to pilfer vehicles during movement with minimal response. The lack of formal protection on most vehicle platforms forced units to improvise in order to secure their vehicles and individual equipment. During the withdrawal and redeployment, each convoy required an armed escort between cargo and personnel redeployment nodes.[38]

Force Protection Materiel

Did convoys have the required materiel to meet the force protection policy's requirements? Military units providing convoy security escort had the required materiel to meet their force protection requirements. However, logistics units struggled to balance convoy security and base security requirements.[39] The requirements and missions exceeded the basic table of organization and equipment baselines, specifically in terms of crew served weapons. During the early 1990s, logistics units had no armored wheeled vehicles or enough ring mounts to properly employ the limited crew served weapons that were also sparsely available. Units took existing

---

[35] Michael Meneghini, phone interview by author, May 30, 2012, Fort Leavenworth, KS.

[36] Robert Baumann, Lawrence Yates, and Washington Versalle, *"My Clan Against The World"*: *U.S. and Coalition Forces In Somalia, 1992-1994* (Fort Leavenworth: Combat Studies Institute, 2004), 121.

[37] David Farlow, e-mail message to author, May 15, 2012, Fort Leavenworth, KS.

[38] Center of Military History, *United States Forces, Somalia: After Action Report and Historical Overview* (Washington: Center of Military History, 2003), 221.

[39] Ibid., 250.

vehicles and enhanced them with sandbag hardening techniques in an attempt to provide an additional layer of security.[40]

Following the August 9, 1993 command-detonated, improvised explosive device attack on a military police convoy that killed four soldiers, the Army addressed the significant force protection shortfall with the rapid fielding of add-on armor kits and eventually the first 50 production models of the M1114 Up-Armored Humvee.[41] Arguably, those platforms arrived too late to make a considerable difference in the operation, but the initiative identified an inherent armored vehicle requirement within the emerging operating environment. However, logistics units would not see the authorization for an armored wheeled vehicle until Operation Iraqi Freedom III in 2005.

A major materiel shortfall within logistics units was the Commercial Utility Cargo Vehicle (CUCV) fleet. The CUCV was a Dodge or General Motors commercial vehicle fielded as an inexpensive augmentation to the aging M151 Jeep fleet. Logisticians serving in Somalia noted that the vehicle was unsuitable for use in combat due to extensive difficulty entering or exiting the vehicle while wearing body armor and other bulky personal gear.[42] Additionally, units were unable to harden the vehicle for protection or add any form of crew-served weapon unless modified with a pedestal that lacked gunner protection.

Force Protection to Sustainment Vehicle Ratio

What was the average force protection to sustainment vehicle ratio? The existing literature does not indicate any consistent force protection ratios during the operation. The 100th Transportation Company, however, embedded two force protection vehicles into each convoy. Regardless of the convoy's size, composition, or mission, the company commander allocated two

---

[40] David Farlow, e-mail message to author, May 15, 2012, Fort Leavenworth, KS.

[41] Richard Killblane, *Circle the Wagons: The History of US Army Convoy Security* (Fort Leavenworth: Combat Studies InstitutePress, 2005), 77.

[42] Alexander Wetzel, "Not Built For Combat," *Army Logistician* (September 1994): 4.

five-ton cargo trucks with a ring-mounted crew served weapon.[43] In some cases, the convoys would have as many as 20 vehicles and still consist of only two security vehicles.

Convoy-related Casualties

How many casualties resulted from sustainment organization-led convoys? No logistics soldiers died during convoys in Somalia. However, four military policemen died on August 8, 1993 while conducting a security patrol along a main supply route.[44] For the entire operation, the United States sustained 43 killed in action due to hostile activities.

Convoy Training

What training did sustainment organizations conduct to prepare for convoys? The Operation Restore Hope After Action Review addressed this topic and specified that logistics units lacked preparation and adequate training to apply the rules of engagement. Even deeper, it identified convoy operations as a weakness.[45] For functional transportation companies, however, existing training programs supported the focus on convoy operations and survivability. Many units lacked veterans of Operation Desert Storm and therefore required aggressive training plans. Prior to deployment notification in late 1992, the 100th Transportation Company trained monthly in a field environment and eventually conducted live fire exercises. The refinement of convoy battle drills prior to deployment facilitated the unit's ability to organize and conduct internally secured convoys immediately upon arrival in country.[46]

Once in Somalia, logistics units developed situational training exercises as a response to the increased ambushes, small arms fire, and rocket propelled grenade attacks. One unit, the 364th Quartermaster Company from Fort Bragg, North Carolina, received notification in July

[43] Michael Meneghini, phone interview by author, May 30, 2012, Fort Leavenworth, KS.

[44] David Farlow, e-mail message to author, May 15, 2012, Fort Leavenworth, KS.

[45] Center of Military History, *United States Forces, Somalia: After Action Report and Historical Overview* (Washington: Center of Military History, 2003), 256.

[46] Michael Meneghini, phone interview by author, May 30, 2012, Fort Leavenworth, KS.

1993 for a September 1993 deployment. The original expectation of a humanitarian assistance mission quickly changed to providing support in a combat environment. Implementing a four-week training plan, the company commander led his 123 soldiers through an aggressive combat focused training exercise focusing efforts on rules of engagement, law of war, reacting to contact, and convoy operations.[47] The unit clearly applied lessons learned and maximized its training opportunities. For military police units providing security near the end of the operation, they focused on their core training programs prior to deployment. Those units refined their techniques for supply route security, reacting to ambush, and convoy operations.[48]

Armed Convoy Security Providers

Who provided armed security for sustainment convoys? Military police and maneuver units provided the preponderance of armed security for logistics convoys during both Operation Restore Hope and Continue Hope. However, some logistics units secured themselves using only internal personnel and equipment during the first six months of the operation.[49] The use of field trains afforded those units the opportunity to conduct that sustainment mission and provide the necessary security. The 300th Military Police Company assumed multiple missions to include convoy escort, main supply route security, and detainee operations.[50]

After the October 3, 1993 raid in Mogadishu where 18 soldiers died, President Clinton announced additional units would arrive to help stabilize the situation. The Commander, U.S. Forces Somalia, requested specific enablers to provide adequate force protection for U.S. logistics convoys. His original request was a mechanized task force consisting of three mechanized infantry companies, a light infantry company, a combat engineer company, a headquarters

---

[47] Larry Naylor, "Supply and Service In Somalia," *Quartermaster Professional Bulletin* (Spring 1994): 26.

[48] David Farlow, e-mail message to author, May 15, 2012, Fort Leavenworth, KS.

[49] Michael Meneghini, phone interview by author, May 30, 2012, Fort Leavenworth, KS.

[50] David Farlow, e-mail message to author, May 15, 2012, Fort Leavenworth, KS.

company with mortars and scouts, and an air cavalry troop consisting of four UH–1 and six OH–58 platforms. Central Command eventually downgraded the request for forces to a single mechanized infantry company, an M1 tank platoon, and a towed artillery battery.[51]

Within the Mogadishu area, OH-58 airframes provided escort by maintaining visibility of the roads ahead of convoys and interdicting when required. However, peak periods allowed for only four convoys a day and limited to the Mogadishu area.[52] The daily convoy requirements in Somalia exceeded the capability to adequately escort and secure with aerial platforms.

Throughout the operation, existing literature indicated no proof of any private security companies or units from the Army National Guard tasked to provide external convoy security. The military police companies and infantry companies from the 10th Mountain Division were the only units to secure convoys as an external capability.[53] The Logistics Support Command facilitated route security by constructing a bypass around Mogadishu.[54] This eliminated the requirement to travel through the city and the Quick Reaction Force conducted daily route clearance patrols to check for land mines or improvised explosive devices.

Summary

The data collected in the structured, focused questions in this case study link to each of the three hypotheses introduced in this monograph's literature review. This summary provides context and interpretation of the direction connections between armed convoy security and Operation Restore Hope as a case study.

---

[51] Center of Military History, *United States Forces, Somalia: After Action Report and Historical Overview* (Washington: Center of Military History, 2003), 120.

[52] Center of Military History, *United States Forces, Somalia: After Action Report and Historical Overview* (Washington: Center of Military History, 2003), 172.

[53] Robert Baumann, Lawrence Yates, and Washington Versalle, *"My Clan Against The World": U.S. and Coalition Forces In Somalia, 1992-1994* (Fort Leavenworth: Combat Studies Institute, 2004), 77.

[54] Center of Military History, *United States Forces, Somalia: After Action Report and Historical Overview* (Washington: Center of Military History, 2003), 134.

Operation Restore Hope had an initial force protection policy that continued to develop as violence escalated and the humanitarian assistance situation deteriorated. Logistics and military police units conducting convoy security operations generally had the required materiel to meet the force protection requirements, but regularly created solutions to mitigate internal shortfalls. Vehicle modernization to adapt to the emerging improvised explosive device threat occurred too late in the operation to make any significant force protection difference. The operation demonstrated inconsistent force protection ratios as many units adhered to the absolute minimum requirement while maximizing the number of transportation vehicles on the road to meet mission requirements. While no logistics units suffered casualties because of convoy operations, the death of four military policemen did initiate the Up-Armored Humvee program and a focus on creating an armored wheeled vehicle platform. Units did conduct pre-deployment and in-theater training to prepare for convoy security operations, however, the level and intensity of training varied resulting in an inconsistent capability when faced with lethal threats in a non-linear combat environment. A combination of military police and internal capability provided armed convoy security. In some cases, the number of logistics convoys exceeded the density of military police available. The use of supply route patrols and security facilitated most convoy operations.

The first hypothesis stated that when a commander uses internally resourced convoy security, then he assumes risk to sustainment capability and mission support. The research suggested that logistics operations required a deliberate balance between convoy operations and base security requirements. Both missions required nearly all available manpower, vehicles, and equipment to attain the necessary tempo. Commanders operated within their limitations and created capability out of hide to meet requirements. When this factor is considered, commanders can embrace those limitations, while simultaneously assuming risk between the competing demands. The evidence suggests that hypothesis one is supported.

The second hypothesis stated that when a commander uses externally resourced convoy security, then he assumes risk to training management, manning, synchronization, materiel, and standardization. The lack of dedicated convoy security units created standardization and synchronization shortfalls. The research indicates the absolute minimum amount of external ground or air assets supported convoy operations resulting in a risk when internal capability could not meet the requirement. External units simply could not meet the requirement to be the sole provider of convoy security for logistics organizations. The evidence suggests that hypothesis two is supported.

The third hypothesis stated that when a commander accepts the status quo for convoy security, then he continues to pull resources out of hide while simultaneously implementing external assets when resourced from a higher headquarters. The various organizations providing security and the overall force protection concept during Operation Restore Hope supported this hypothesis. The research clearly identifies instances where resources came out of hide, creating internal capability shortfalls, while also employing a slice of security from military police organizations pushing the limits of their capability. This fundamentally created an imbalanced approach towards convoy security as a whole. With limitations, some logistics units received external security, and some did not. This inconsistency ultimately forces a logistics commander to assume he will not have external security and thus inherently pull from internal capability. The evidence suggests that hypothesis three is supported.

Convoys During Operation Iraqi Freedom

Operation Iraqi Freedom, an enduring conflict that lasted from March 20, 2003 to September 30, 2010, followed a complex path of military actions. Initially a major engagement between coalition forces and Saddam Hussein's military power, the war rapidly evolved into a sectarian violence filled counterinsurgency with thousands of casualties. The U.S. Army transformed into a brigade-centric organization in response to the changing environment and long-term commitment.

The purpose of this section is to identify the war's effect on convoy operations and the capacity for logistics organizations to adequately adapt to the constantly changing force protection requirements posed by a volatile and elusive enemy. This specific case study provided an opportunity to examine both major combat operations and counterinsurgency warfare under a single named operation, an aspect not demonstrated in the previous case study covering Operation Restore Hope in Somalia. The basic conduct of ground convoys during this period proved to challenge the Army's organizational and training structure beyond any previously recorded operation.

Operation Iraqi Freedom serves as an excellent example for reviewing armed convoy security due to the diverse nature of both combat and sustainment operations. The Army's drastic transition from supply point logistics to distribution based logistics occurred during this period. Although planners laid the groundwork for the transition prior to 2003, the nature of this major combat operation necessitated a quicker and more complete transformation.[55] Dealing with a noncontiguous battlefield and nonpermissive environment, the previous mindset of building mountains of logistics shifted to enabling materiel visibility and velocity management in conjunction with a solid ground, air, and sea transportation network.

Ground force modernization prior to Operation Iraqi Freedom allowed for unparalleled operational tempo during both the invasion in March 2003 and throughout operations over the following seven years. Improvements in distribution capability and technology created "three dimensional" logistics that offered commanders and planners real-time visibility of materiel

---

[55] Timothy Reese and Donald Wright, *On Point II: Transition To The New Campaign* (Fort Leavenworth: Combat Studies Institute Press, 2008), 490.

movement.[56] However, that tempo developed situations where logistics and support forces operated independently and regularly beyond the scope of security expected within the flanks and rear areas in maneuver operations.[57]

The war's initial phase, the invasion, lasted from March 19, 2003 to April 9, 2003. In this short period, a coalition consisting primarily of the United States, United Kingdom, and Australia moved north from Kuwait to Baghdad with the objective of disarming Iraq of weapons of mass destruction and ending Saddam Hussein's role as Iraq's leader, thus ending decades of tyranny. By 2005, the Central Intelligence Agency reported that the coalition discovered no weapons of mass destruction in Iraq, despite the country's collapse. Saddam Hussein, sentenced to death by a jury, died after hanging in December 2006.

Following nearly three painful years of attempts to stabilize Iraq, the multinational force refocused efforts in 2007 to defeat the insurgent threat. Escalation of violence among sectarian groups facilitated the swift emergence of Al Qaeda elements that targeted coalition forces and the civilian population. The counterinsurgency focus increased the U.S. military footprint in Iraq by five brigade combat teams. Charged with executing a strategy to help the Iraqi security forces clear and secure neighborhoods, the surge of units supported the establishment of conditions to posture reconciliation between political and ethnic groups. Ultimately, it created the opportunity for the overall withdrawal of American forces.

In early 2009, newly elected president Barack Obama announced the end of combat operations in Iraq by August 31, 2010 and a transition to an advisory mission, Operation New Dawn. Tens of thousands of military personnel and associated equipment withdrew from Iraq by

---

[56] Anthony Cordesman, *The Iraq War: Strategy, Tactics, and Military Lessons* (Washington: CSIS, 2003), 205.

[57] Ibid., 206.

the end of 2011. Concurrently, the advisory and assistance mission continued efforts to develop Iraqi security forces despite violent acts towards security forces and civilians.

Force Protection Policy

Did the operation have an overall force protection policy for ground movement? As the operation evolved, force protection policies developed in response to the enemy actions. Although the specific force protection requirements are classified, available literature suggests minimum policies during specific periods of the operation. In 2004, U.S. Army Transportation Corps historian Richard Killblane noted that there was no requirement for armor on convoy gun trucks. However, each convoy required a minimum of two crew-served weapons, regardless of the weapon's caliber.[58] Later, in 2005, battle space owners within Iraq established criteria for convoys to operate on specific routes. For example, routes identified with an amber safety rating required an armed convoy escort, but those routes categorized with red status would only see combat arms units.[59] By 2009, all convoys required a minimum of three armored wheeled vehicles with a minimum crew of three personnel and a crew served weapon per vehicle. This limitation for sustainment organizations crossing brigade or divisional boundaries while conducting throughput distribution operations further stressed the numerous manning and equipment shortfalls.

Force Protection Materiel

Did convoys have the required materiel to meet the force protection policy's requirements? During the initial period of Operation Iraqi Freedom, convoys lacked the required materiel to meet force protection policy requirements. In 2003 as units conducted the initial invasion, organic equipment, to include wheeled vehicles such as the non-armored High Mobility

---

[58] Timothy Reese and Donald Wright, *On Point II: Transition To The New Campaign* (Fort Leavenworth: Combat Studies Institute Press, 2008), 507.

[59] Robert Gillespie, "Route Ownership Versus Route Concession" *Armor* (September 2005): 18.

Multipurpose Wheeled Vehicle, provided the primary ground movement capability for logistics units. However, some units' basic equipment authorization still created shortfalls when convoys and other sustainment operations developed. The 3rd Corps Support Command launched into Iraq in March 2003 with 20 percent of the assets required to conduct operations. Additionally, other logistics units struggled to assemble convoys with adequate command, control, communications, computers, and information equipment necessary for extended length operations.[60] However, as national attention drew to this problem, the Army mitigated materiel shortfalls through acquisition and both informal and formal vehicle armor modifications. The 3rd COSCOM faced a limiting factor of only one radio for every five vehicles.[61] The shortfalls—mostly in the form of vehicle armor—took approximately three years to mitigate and provide both the quality and density necessary to meet the emerging and evolving threat in Iraq.

The diverse sustainment vehicle fleet challenged the Army's efforts to modernize and provide adequate armor for convoy protection. The "360-degree Iraqi insurgency" forced units seeking survival to develop internal solutions.[62] Several units, prior to receiving formal armor plating kits or commercial, mine-resistant vehicles between 2003 and 2005, scrounged and developed what will forever be known as "hillbilly armor" to informally meet their vehicle force protection requirements.[63] By 2006, the Army Materiel Command assembled "add on armor" kits for the entire HMMWV fleet in response to the improvised explosive device threat and HMMWV vulnerabilities.

By 2009, the Theater Provided Equipment program provided a massive fleet of armored wheeled vehicles to include multiple Mine Resistant Ambush Protected variants. The effort

---

[60] Timothy Reese and Donald Wright, *On Point II: Transition To The New Campaign* (Fort Leavenworth: Combat Studies Institute Press, 2008), 501.

[61] Ibid., 499.

[62] Timothy Reese and Donald Wright, *On Point II: Transition To The New Campaign* (Fort Leavenworth: Combat Studies Institute Press, 2008), *509.*

[63] Ibid., 510.

ensured soldiers conducted missions with that best armored protection posture available to the U.S. Forces-Iraq.

Force Protection to Sustainment Vehicle Ratio

What was the average force protection to sustainment vehicle ratio? The force protection vehicle to sustainment vehicle ratio varied, depending on the type of convoy operation conducted. With an unequal balance of pure military convoys and military mixed with host nation or contracted vehicles, the force protection ratio saw an extreme range. During the first few years of the war, common practice was for a single, armed military vehicle providing protection for every three host nation support or contracted vehicles.[64] The 7th Transportation Battalion, in 2004, employed a ratio of one force protection vehicle to every five military-pure logistics vehicles.[65] As the theater matured, the battalion embedded commercial, contracted logistics vehicles and allocated one military force protection vehicle for every 10 "white" vehicles. Later, the force protection posture eventually allowed for weapons within those vehicles, thus increasing the defensive capability within each convoy.

Mission requirements led to convoys that pushed the force protection ratio beyond what is logically acceptable. The 7th Transportation Battalion attempted to keep its convoys under 25 total vehicles to maintain maximum control and protection based on available assets. One report from 2005 indicated a ratio of three force protection vehicles to secure a 30-vehicle movement of commercial, contracted trucks in northern Iraq.[66] As Operation Iraqi Freedom ended in 2010, security force requirements exceeded capability and convoy size increased, regularly up to 55 vehicles in the United States Division-North area as part of the hub and spoke distribution plan.

---

[64] Timothy Reese and Donald Wright, *On Point II: Transition To The New Campaign* (Fort Leavenworth: Combat Studies Institute Press, 2008), 504.

[65] George Akin, personal interview with the U.S. Army Combat Studies Institute's Operational Leadership Experiences program, November 2, 2005, Fort Bragg, NC.

[66] Timothy Goad, Personal Experience Paper, United States Sergeants Major Academy, January 9, 2010.

Convoy-related Casualties

How many casualties resulted from sustainment organization-led convoys? Between March 2003 and August 2010, 124 logistics soldiers died because of enemy action during sustainment convoys. According to the Defense Manpower Data Center, 66 percent were victims of improvised explosive devices and the remaining 34 percent resulted from small arms fire.[67] With air and ground evacuation measures combined with advanced medical capability across the operational environment, the ability to save lives increased significantly over previous operations. This fact is evident when the number of personnel wounded in action is considered.

Additionally, as Operation Iraqi Freedom evolved and the reliance on civilian contractors expanded at unprecedented levels, civilian contractor casualties increased. Existing data shows 468 civilian contractor casualties during the operation. Within than number, 155, or 33 percent were a result of attacks on convoy operations.[68]

Convoy Training

What training did sustainment organizations conduct to prepare for convoys? Each unit's component—reserve or active—drove the level of training conducted in preparation for convoy mission. For reserve component units, many organizations in the early years of the operation found themselves slated for combat training center rotations and trained directly with active duty brigade combat teams destined for Iraq. The unique backgrounds of Army Reserve and Army National Guard personnel created, in many cases, creative solutions when training opportunities

---

[67] Ad Hoc report from the Defense Manpower Data Center generated on March 13, 2012. The report listed all hostile casualties with their associated service, component, occupational specialty, and cause of death during Operations Iraqi Freedom and Enduring Freedom.

[68] Iraq Coalition Casualties: Contractors. http://icasualties.org/iraq/contractors.aspx (accessed May 16, 2012).

did not exist. The age and experience, coupled with cohesiveness, fostered a "get it done" approach to make up for training inconsistencies.[69]

For active units, multiple training options existed. For example, the 204th Brigade Support Battalion coordinated initial convoy security detachment training through a Mobile Training Team brought in from Fort Knox, Kentucky.[70] This institutional training supported the organization's collective training at the National Training Center during the 2nd Heavy Brigade Combat Team, 4th Infantry Division's mission rehearsal exercise prior to deployment in 2009. This proved critical as the battalion regularly faced more limitations with trained personnel than wheeled vehicles to transport supplies.

Armed Convoy Security Providers

Who provided armed security for sustainment convoys? Operation Iraqi Freedom exploited all opportunities for armed convoy security. Both internal and external organizations provided security in addition to host nation and private military companies. As sustainment organizations experienced manning shortfalls, maneuver units augmented the convoy security tasks.[71] Reconfiguring some maneuver units, such as field artillery battalions, into convoy security units increased capability and maximized available forces.[72] One Heavy Equipment Transport (HET) company from the Army National Guard received infantry soldiers from 3rd Brigade, 4th Infantry Division to create its internal security platoon.[73]

---

[69] George Akin, personal interview with the U.S. Army Combat Studies Institute's Operational Leadership Experiences program, November 2, 2005, Fort Bragg, NC.

[70] Michael Siegl, "Sustaining a BCT In Southern Iraq," *Army Sustainment* 42, no. 6 (November 2010): 29.

[71] Timothy Reese and Donald Wright, *On Point II: Transition To The New Campaign* (Fort Leavenworth: Combat Studies Institute Press, 2008), 498.

[72] Dave Vesper, personal interview with the U.S. Army Combat Studies Institute's Operational Leadership Experiences program, January 19, 2011, Fort Leavenworth, KS.

[73] Kenneth Blasko, Personal Experience Paper, United States Sergeants Major Academy, September 3, 2006.

More than 305 airmen from the U.S. Air Force's 732nd Expeditionary Logistics Readiness Squadron provided logistical support to Joint Base Balad, but concurrently operated gun trucks in direct support of the 181st Transportation Battalion's mission in northern Iraq. The Air Force had not conducted this type of integrated armed convoy security support since the Vietnam War.[74]

Sustainment organizations employed all three aspects of convoy security during Operation Iraqi Freedom. Resurrecting the Vietnam War gun truck concept, the 3rd COSCOM established internal convoy security elements to meet the minimum convoy force protection requirements; two High Mobility Multi-Purpose Wheeled Vehicles with whatever crew-served weapon systems were available.[75] Ironically, as the war became a counterinsurgency and the civilian contractor footprint expanded, several transportation companies supplemented their support battalion's internal convoy requirements by creating gun truck platoons with improvised armor plating and crew-served weapons. The benefit of this internal capability is the creation of continuity between those conducting the convoys and those protecting it. However, as one sustainment brigade commander pointed out, creating this capability from within pushed the envelope, as the next higher headquarters would task the brigade based on platforms available and not personnel available.

As discussed in the previous research question, external maneuver units supported numerous logistics organizations through task organized convoy escort teams. This external effort afforded logistics battalions the opportunity to meet the balance of their supply, maintenance, and distribution requirements without sacrificing a capability for convoy security. Another external convoy capability was the use of contractors operating logistics equipment. Eventually armed, the

---

[74] Lance Cheung, "Road Warriors," *Airman* (Spring 2005): 15.

[75] Timothy Reese and Donald Wright, *On Point II: Transition To The New Campaign* (Fort Leavenworth: Combat Studies Institute Press, 2008), 504.

civilian augmentation placed logistics soldiers in the security role while the contractors operated tractors pulling flatbed trailers of cargo or tankers of fuel.

Field Manual Interim 4-93.2, *The Sustainment Brigade*, illustrates corridor security as one of the three layers of tactical convoy physical security.[76] Existing literature does not indicate this was ever the sole source of physical security. However, during the invasion in 2003, V Corps tasked three divisions and one armored cavalry regiment to secure supply routes from Kuwait north to Baghdad. Over the following seven years, battle space owners provided varying levels of route security within their areas of operation.

Summary

To summarize the collection of data generated by the focused research questions in the case study, this section connects the data to each hypothesis introduced in the literature review section. This approach provides context and linkage to the overall thesis by interpreting it through the lens of each convoy security hypothesis.

Operation Iraqi Freedom had an overall force protection policy, but it varied through time and location. Logistics units initially lacked adequate materiel to meet force protection requirements but eventually improvised with existing equipment until modernization efforts reached the theater. Force protection ratios between armed security vehicles and logistics vehicles remained unbalanced nearly all seven years and the ratio ultimately increased during the drawdown from 2009 to 2010. The Army logistics community suffered 124 casualties during convoy operations from 2003 to 2010 due to small arms fire and improvised explosive devices. Essentially all units managed to conduct pre-deployment training and training in theater, however, the home station training lacked the environment to simulate the scope of the tactics, techniques, and procedures required in Iraq. A wide variety of units provided convoy security to

---

[76] Department of the Army, *Field Manual Interim 4-93.2 The Sustainment Brigade* (Washington: Government Printing Office, 2009), B-72.

include organic capability, contractors, external maneuver units from the active and reserve components, and even the U.S. Air Force. Finally, sustainment organizations received support from all three layers of the doctrinal convoy security model to include internal protection, external security, and corridor security.

The first hypothesis states that when a commander uses internally resourced convoy security, then he assumes risk to sustainment capability and mission support. The research suggested that while internal convoy security increases training and teamwork opportunities, it does stretch mission support and capability. However, that same internal flexibility reduces support constraints posed by poor external security synchronization. Finally, the lack of dedicated armored convoy escort vehicles within logistics units causes a significant planning limitation. Thus, the evidence suggests that hypothesis one is supported.

The second hypothesis states that when a commander uses externally resourced convoy security, then he assumes risk to training management, manning, synchronization, materiel, and standardization. The evidence supports this hypothesis in two fundamental ways. First, by tasking external organizations to provide convoy security, that organization can focus exclusively on training, manning, and equipping without logistics support mission constraints. Second, it allows logistics units to focus on functional logistics tasks such as supply, maintenance, or health services support without committing extraneous capability to serve as internal convoy security during distribution operations.

The third hypothesis states that when a commander accepts the status quo for convoy security, then he continues to pull resources out of hide while simultaneously implementing external assets when resourced from a higher headquarters. This hypothesis is driven by the element of the unknown; a logistics commander deploying to Iraq may not know if planners factored external convoy security elements. Additionally, this gap forced commanders to create capability from within existing formations already charged with a logistics mission, thus eliminating any redundant support capability. Lastly, the diversity of external security enablers

34

combined with internal capability leads to inconsistent standards if the enablers do not remain consistently embedded with the logistics unit. Thus, the evidence suggests that hypothesis three is supported.

Findings and Analysis

This section will assist the reader in moving beyond the initial impressions of the topic of armed convoy security and improve the likelihood that the evidence presented is reliable. The use of a comparison matrix will illustrate patterns across the three case studies and the research questions to ultimately validate the hypotheses. When the findings conflict, however, this analysis will dig deeper to identify and explain the sources of conflict in the research.

Findings

In the findings discussion, three steps encompass the process. First, the comparison matrix, Table 1, provides a visualization of each research question and the corresponding summary of data for each case study. Second, restated research questions ensure standardization across the findings. Finally, highlights of each case study's response provide justification for the findings and transition to the analysis portion.

Findings		
Question	Operation Restore Hope	Operation Iraqi Freedom
1. Did the operation have an overall force protection policy for ground movement?	Yes	Yes
2. Did convoys have the required materiel to meet the force protection policy's requirements?	Yes	No
3. What was the average force protection to sustainment vehicle ratio?	Varied	Varied
4. How many casualties resulted from sustainment organization-led convoys?	Zero	124 KIA
5. What training did sustainment organizations conduct to prepare for convoys?	Minimal	Evolved to adapt
6. Who provided armed security for sustainment convoys?	Internal & External	Internal & External

Table 1. Case Study Findings

Research Question 1: Did the operation have an overall force protection policy for ground movement? During Operation Restore Hope, a force protection policy existed but did not initially require any crew served weapons, only a minimum number of vehicles. As the operation progressed and violence increased, crew served weapons became a force protection requirement for convoys. For Operation Iraqi Freedom, a progressing and evolving policy morphed from essentially nothing up to a minimum of three armored vehicles each with three personnel and a minimum of three crew served weapons.

Research Question 2: Did convoys have the required materiel to meet the force protection policy's requirements? Forces conducting operations in Somalia during Operation Restore Hope had the minimum amount of equipment required to meet the force protection policy while also meeting other force protection requirements. During Operation Iraqi Freedom, logistics units did not have the required force protection material on tables of organization and equipment. However, the creation of Theater Provided Equipment program generated the right mix of equipment in Iraq to meet the requirements, despite no alignment with authorization documents. By 2010, units were conducting convoy operations with the required equipment.

Research Question 3: What was the average force protection to sustainment vehicle ratio? No consistent force protection to sustainment vehicle ratio existed during Operation Restore Hope other than units meeting the minimum force protection policy of two vehicles. For Operation Iraqi Freedom, however, the density of logistics convoys created massive variations in the ratio. With convoys as few as 10 vehicles or as large as 50, the composition between commercial and military vehicles created no identifiable standard.

Research Question 4: How many casualties resulted from sustainment organization-led convoys? During Operation Restore Hope, sustainment organization-led convoys sustained zero casualties. However, during the significantly longer Operation Iraqi Freedom, 124 military personnel were killed in action during convoy operations. Additionally, at least 155 civilian contractors died as a result of enemy aggression towards convoys.

Research Question 5: What training did sustainment organizations conduct to prepare for convoys? For units deploying to Somalia, existing literature indicates that sustainment units failed to conduct convoy and rules of engagement training. However, transportation commanders stated they did, in fact, conduct convoy operations training, reacting to contact, and live fire exercises prior to deployment. Additionally, the units providing convoy security also conducted convoy and security training in concert with their doctrinal training plans. During Operation Iraqi Freedom, training across the spectrum of units, to include logistics, evolved significantly between 2003 and 2010. During the earliest periods of the war, non-logistics units tasked with convoy security missions found themselves without preparation. However, by the last few years of the operation, nearly all deploying units conducted convoy live fire exercises to meet standard mission requirements.

Research Question 6: Who provided armed security for sustainment convoys? The two operations are very similar with this research question in that a combination of internal and external elements provided armed security for sustainment convoys. During Operation Restore Hope, military police units provided the preponderance of escort support when available and units without coverage created an internal capability to complete mission requirements and meet force protection policies. Similarly, in Iraq, when sustainment units lacked an external escort capability such as a maneuver unit or National Guard unit, they reorganized organic equipment and personnel to task organize internal convoy security elements.

Analysis

In the analysis discussion, four steps encompass the process. First, the comparison matrix, Table 2, provides a visualization of each hypothesis and its stance as supported or not supported in each case study after analyzing the research questions in the findings section. Next, restated hypotheses ensure standardization across the findings. Then, a discussion on the highlights of each hypothesis provides justification for the analysis. Finally, the analysis concludes by determining if each hypothesis does support or does not support each case study.

Analysis		
Hypothesis	Operation Restore Hope	Operation Iraqi Freedom
1. When a commander uses internally resourced convoy security, then he assumes risk to sustainment capability and mission support.	Supported	Supported
2. When a commander uses externally resourced convoy security, then he assumes risk to training management, manning, synchronization, materiel, and standardization.	Supported	Supported
3. When a commander accepts the status quo for convoy security, then he continues to pull resources out of hide while simultaneously implementing external assets when resourced from a higher headquarters.	Supported	Supported

Table 2. Hypothesis Analysis

Restated Hypothesis 1: When a commander uses internally resourced convoy security, then he assumes risk to sustainment capability and mission support. The findings from both case studies support this hypothesis. Specifically, evidence from operations in both Somalia and Iraq indicate that commanders deliberately reduced capability in other areas in order to create internal convoy security enablers. This was due, in many cases, to the progressing force protection requirements as threats in both operations emerged in a non-linear manner. The traditional rear area security simply did not exist and without some capability, logistics units conducting convoys in semi-permissive environments could not accomplish their missions.

Restated Hypothesis 2: When a commander uses externally resourced convoy security, then he assumes risk to training management, manning, synchronization, materiel, and standardization. Again, with this hypothesis, both case studies support the argument. In Somalia, the lack of dedicated units providing habitual convoy security created synchronization and standardization shortfalls. This fostered a lack of connection between the logistics unit and the units providing security. There simply were not enough military police units to secure all logistics convoys. In Iraq, the much larger scope of the environment further complicated convoy operations in general. Eventually the resourcing of dedicated external convoy security units alleviated the manning, synchronization, materiel, and standardization shortfalls initially experienced during the first few years of the operation. However, commanders still assume risk to training management when units were unable to train together either at a combat training center or at home station prior to deployment.

Restated Hypothesis 3: When a commander accepts the status quo for convoy security, then he continues to pull resources out of hide while simultaneously implementing external assets when resourced from a higher headquarters. Evidence from both operations supports this hypothesis. Based on the tactics, techniques, and procedures developed in both Somalia and Iraq, a commander will instinctively create capability regardless of what a higher headquarters may or may not resource. Further, when conditions exist where casualties are imminent, leaders will not wait for an external manning or equipping solution.

Recommendations and Conclusion

Recommendations

This monograph's primary argument posited that when externally resourced convoy escorts are used, then a sustainment brigade commander assumes risk with his distribution mission, and when internally resourced convoy escort is constructed and employed, a sustainment brigade commander has complete control over convoy unity of command, home station training, and convoy cohesion. As the evidence supporting each hypothesis indicates, sustainment units will accept whatever external asset is resourced, or they will create capability internally with a deliberate decision making process.

The analysis leads to three recommendations for improving the Army's armed convoy security requirement. Each recommendation assumes alignment with a functional sustainment brigade.

First, the Army should create a modular Convoy Security Company for each sustainment brigade. The key task of this company would be to provide convoy security for a CSSB aligned under each sustainment brigade. Their purpose would be to ensure maximum, unconstrained mobility and force protection when operating within and outside of divisional boundaries. This organization would retain four functional security platoons with armored wheeled vehicles. Each platoon would align to support a single CSSB in order to provide maximum integration and training to ensure mission success.

Next, the Army should create habitual maneuver unit augmentation and alignment. This measure would link a sustainment brigade and its subordinate CSSBs with a maneuver unit. Characterized by its manning, this approach would align Soldiers from maneuver units with equipment organic to CSSBs such as armored wheeled vehicles and crew served weapons. Employing this technique would create a connection between the logistics commander and his security force during both training and operations.

Finally, the third recommendation is to maintain the status quo. Clearly, as demonstrated in the two case studies, small units will embrace creativity and make missions occur with or without proper resources. However, as the evidence suggests, commanders assume risk to mission accomplishment with all options.

Conclusion

American military theorist Dennis Hart Mahan believed few operations were more hazardous than convoys and therefore required commanders to anticipate the enemy.[77] The findings of this study build upon two decades of armed convoy security operations observations and research. This monograph revealed a common trend between two unique case studies that a shortfall fundamentally exists. However, logistics units will continue to accept and execute their missions as directed. Operational planners must consider all aspects of convoy security during mission planning. Understanding the gap between requirement and shortfall—sustainment brigades conducting armed escorted convoys without internal capability—a degree of integration

---

[77] D.H. Mahan, *An Elementary Treatise On Advanced-Guard* (New York: John Wiley, 1861), paragraph 419.

must occur to prevent the enemy from anticipating potentially unsynchronized and untrained logistics units.

Embracing the realities of ad hoc convoy security solutions from the past 20 years requires a sweeping change across the DOTMLPF to prepare for the future environment. This study concludes that internally resourced capability provides commanders the best options for securing their inherently tasked mission, logistics convoys. The adoption of in-progress solutions such as the Up-Armored Humvee near the end of Operation Restore Hope or the MRAP family of vehicles near the last third of Operation Iraqi Freedom demonstrate great initiatives, but the fact remains that logistics units had those requirements long before the demand.

Bibliography

Baumann, Robert F., Lawrence A. Yates, and Washington F. Versalle. *"My Clan Against The World": U.S. and Coalition Forces In Somalia, 1992-1994.* Fort Leavenworth, Kansas: Combat Studies Institute, US Army Command and General Staff College, 2004.

Bennett, Andrew, and Alexander L. George. *Case Studies and Theory Development In The Social Sciences.* Cambridge, Massachussetts: MIT Press, 2005.

Center of Military History. *United States Forces, Somalia: After Action Report and Historical Overview.* Washington, DC: Center of Military History, 2003.

Cheung, Lance. "Road Warriors." *Airman,* Spring 2005: 14-19.

Cholek, Brandon C., and Matthew A. Anderson Sr. "Distribution-Based Logistics in Operation Iraqi Freedom." *Army Logistician* 39, no. 2 (March 2007): 2-8.

Cordesman, Anthony H. *The Iraq War : Strategy, Tactics, and Military Lessons.* Washington, D.C.: CSIS, 2003.

Department of Defense. *Joint Publication 1-02, Department of Defense Dictionary of Military and Associated Terms.* Washington, D.C.: Government Printing Office, 2010, Amended Through 15 January 2012.

Department of the Army. *Field Manual 3-90, Tactics.* Washington, D.C.: Government Printing Office, 2001.

—. *Field Manual 4-01.45, Tactical Convoy Operations.* Washington, D.C.: Government Printing Office, 2009.

—. *Field Manual Interim 4-93-2, The Sustainment Brigade.* Washington, D.C.: Government Printing Office, 2009.

Dominique, Dean J. "Gun Trucks: A Vietnam Innovation Returns." *Army Logistician* 38, no. 1 (January 2006): 46-49.

Gillespie, Robert B. "Route Ownership Versus Route Concession." *Armor,* September 2005: 18-20.

Godfrey, Frederick V. "The Keys To A Successful Combat Logistics Patrol." *Army Logistician* 38, no. 4 (July 2006): 28-33.

Harris, Michael J., and Eric P. Roby. "Echelons-Above-Brigade Convoy Management in Afghanistan." *Army Sustainment* 42, no. 6 (November 2010): 16.

Iraq Coalition Casualties: Contractors. http://icasualties.org/iraq/contractors.aspx (accessed May 16, 2012).

Killblane, Richard E. *Circle the Wagons: The History of US Army Convoy Security.* Fort Leavenworth, Kansas: Combat Studies Institute Press, 2005.

Kough, Kris. "Share the Road: Convoy Escort." *Army Sustainment* 42, no. 3 (May 2010): 23-24.

Lacroix, Everett. "Adding MRAPs To Transportation Companies." *Army Sustainment* 43, no. 5 (September 2011): 26-27.

Layer, Brian. "Some Principles of Convoy Operations In Operations Other Than War." *Defense Technical Information Center.* December 17, 1993. http://www.dtic.mil/cgi-bin/GetTRDoc?AD=ADA288865 (accessed April 1, 2012).

Macgregor, Douglas A. *Transformation Under Fire : Revolutionizing How America Fights.* Westport, Connecticut: Praeger, 2003.

Mahan, D. H. *An Elementary Treatise on Advanced-Guard, Out-Post, and Detachment Service of Troops, and the Manner of Posting and Handling Them in Presence of an Enemy. With a Historical Sketch of the Rise and Progress of Tactics.* New York: John Wiley, 1861.

Naylor, Larry. "Supply and Service In Somalia." *Quartermaster Professional Bulletin*, Spring 1994: 26-27.

Page, Timothy N., and Mark J. Weinerth. "Top Flite: How One BSB Secured Logistics Convoys In Iraq." *Army Logistician* 41, no. 3 (May 2009): 28-31.

Perry, Dustin. *'Hodgepodge' Convoy Escort Platoon Comes Together To Get Job Done.* February 20, 2007. http://www.nationalguard.mil/news/archives/2007/02/022007-Hodgepodge.aspx (accessed April 11, 2012).

Peterson, Gregory. "Tactical Convoy Planning For Sustainers." *Army Logistician* 41, no. 5 (September 2009): 46-50.

Reese, Timothy R., and Donald P. Wright. *On Point II: Transition To The New Campaign.* Fort Leavenworth, Kansas: Combat Studies Institute Press, 2008.

Reyes, Julio J. "Forward Support Company Operations In Haiti." *Army Sustainment* 42, no. 4 (July 2010): 6-9.

Rossi, Daniel T. "The Logistics Convoy: A Combat Operation." *Army Logistician* 37, no. 1 (January 2005): 38-40.

Ruths, John M. "A Paradigm Shift At NTC: CSSBs That Think "Inside The Box"." *Army Sustainment* 42, no. 3 (May 2010): 2-6.

Siegl, Michael B. "Sustaining A BCT In Southern Iraq." *Army Sustainment* 42, no. 6 (November 2010): 28-31.

Walsh, Shawn P. "More Tooth For The Tail: The Right Stuff For CSS Operations." *Army Logistician* 36, no. 1 (January 2004): 10-13.

War Department: Office of the Chief of Staff. *Field Service Regulation, United States Army.* Washington, DC: Government Printing Office, 1914. Corrected to 15 April 1917.

Wetzel, Alexander C. "Not Built For Combat." *Army Logistician*, September 1994: 3-4.

Ziv, Eyal. "Logistics In Asymmetric Conflicts." *Army Sustainment* 44, no. 1 (January 2012): 46-48.